Publisher's note:
This modern version has been updated from the original text. Words, expressions, and sentence structure have been revised for clarity and readability.

All rights are reserved. No part of this revised text may be reproduced or distributed without the publisher's explicit written consent.

AbidingInk.org

Version: 2025-08-09

THE CURE OF MELANCHOLY AND EXCESSIVE SORROW
By Faith and Medicine

RICHARD BAXTER (1682)
REVISED TO MODERN ENGLISH (2025)

*This text was originally titled
"The Cure of Melancholy and Overmuch Sorrow, by Faith and Physic."*

Prelude		 1
1.	When Sorrow Is Excessive	 6
2.	The Causes and Cure of Melancholy	 11
3.	The Signs of Debilitating Melancholy	 13
4.	Possession by the Devil	 17
5.	Other Usual Causes	 21
6.	Melancholy and Sin for Christians	 26
7.	Guidelines for Peace	 38
8.	For Those Troubled by Sin	 45
9.	The Responsibility of Friends and Relatives	 56
10.	Medical Care	 60

Prelude

"Lest perhaps such a one be swallowed up with too much sorrow." 2 Corinthians 2:7

What are the best ways to prevent melancholy and excessive sorrow?

Because a sermon is brief, I will not take time to explain the context or to investigate whether the person mentioned here is the same one condemned for incest in 1 Corinthians 5:1 or someone else. I will not consider whether Chrysostom had good reason to think this was a teacher of the church, or whether he became one after his sin. Nor will I address whether the recent expositor is correct in suggesting that he was one of the bishops of Achaia, and that a synod of bishops was to excommunicate him. That expositor further argued that this very congregation had a bishop who was to be excommunicated, and that the people should not have followed or supported such a teacher. He believed it would not have been a schism or sinful separation to have forsaken him.

What I intend to do now is to explain this last clause of the verse. It provides the reason why the censured sinner, being penitent, should be forgiven and comforted — namely, "lest perhaps such a one be swallowed up with too much sorrow." This includes three doctrines, which I will address together:

1. Sorrow, even for sin, can be excessive.

2. Excessive sorrow can overwhelm a person.

3. Therefore, it must be resisted and alleviated by necessary comfort, both from others and from ourselves.

In discussing these points, I will follow this order:

1. I will show you when sorrow is excessive.

2. How excessive sorrow overwhelms a person.

3. What its causes are.

4. What the cure is.

It is well known that excessive sorrow for sin is not the common experience of the world. A dull, hardened disposition is the typical cause of most people's downfall. The plague of a hard heart and a seared conscience prevents many from feeling any proper sense of sin, danger, or misery, or from grasping the lasting concerns of their guilty souls.

A dead sleep in sin deprives most people of their ability to sense and understand. They perform outward acts of religion as if in a dream. For instance, others may present them to God in baptism and they themselves profess to uphold that vow. They attend church, recite the creed, the Lord's Prayer, and the commandments. They receive the Lord's Supper. They do all this as if asleep.

They convince themselves that sin is the most detestable thing to God and harmful to humanity, yet they live in it with pleasure and stubbornness. They believe they repent when, in reality, no persuasion will make them abandon it; and meanwhile they despise those who would help them. They imagine they are not as bad as those who would see genuine sorrow for the past, any real awareness of their present state, or any sincere resolution to live anew and holy.

They must believe there is a judgment, a heaven, and a hell — wouldn't these matters affect them more if they were awake? Would they be so consumed by worldly things and hardly think of eternity if they were truly sensible? How sleepily and thoughtlessly they think, speak, and hear about Christ's great work of redemption, about the need of justifying and sanctifying grace, and about the joys and miseries of the next life — and yet they claim to believe these things.

When we preach or speak to them about the most important matters — with the greatest clarity, plainness, and earnestness we can muster — we are often addressing the dead or those who are asleep. They have ears, yet do not hear; nothing penetrates their hearts. One would think that a person who reads Scripture and believes both the everlasting glory promised and the dreadful punishment threatened — the necessity of holiness for salvation, the need of a Savior to deliver us from sin and hell, and how certain and near our transition to the unseen world is — would be moved to account for such overwhelming truths.

Yet most people regard these matters so little that they have neither the time nor the heart to consider them as their concern. They hear of them as if they came from a distant land in which they have no interest and which they never expect to see. Yes, by their senseless neglect and worldly minds, one would think they were asleep or jesting when they confess that they must die. When they lay friends in the grave and see skulls and bones unearthed, they act as if they had been dreaming all along or do not believe their turn is near.

If we could awaken sinners, they would come to their senses, change how they think about these significant matters, and show it by a different life. Surely an awakened reason could never be so deceived and intoxicated as the ungodly world appears. But God has a day of awakening for all, and He will make even the most senseless soul feel — whether by grace or by punishment.

Because a hardened heart is so significant a part of the malady and misery of the unregenerate — and because a soft, tender heart is a key aspect of the new nature promised by Christ — many awakened souls undergoing conversion believe they can never have too much sorrow. They fear only hard-heartedness and do not suspect that sorrow itself can become excessive.

Indeed, although many causes contribute to their state, when sorrow concerns sin they embrace it as a necessary duty and fail to recognize the danger of excess. Some suppose that those most filled with doubts, fears, and complaints — those who speak almost solely of their discomforts — are the best Christians. This is a significant misunderstanding.

Sorrow becomes excessive when it rests on a mistaken cause. Any sorrow is too much when it is undeserved; great sorrow is excessive when the cause warrants only a lesser response. If someone believes they have failed in a duty that is not actually theirs, and then grieves over it, that sorrow is excessive because it is unwarranted and born of error.

I have known many who were deeply troubled because they could not reach the level of meditation they believed required, despite lacking the time or ability. Many are distressed because they feel unable to correct others' sins, when wise instruction and discretion would have been more fitting than reproof. Others are troubled because, in their work and daily activities, they think of anything but God—as if external responsibilities should never involve any thought of Him.

Superstition often breeds such sorrows when people invent religious duties God never intended and then feel guilty for failing to fulfill them. Many troubled souls are misled by false beliefs and told they are on the wrong path, which drives them to accept error as necessary truth. This can throw them into confusing dilemmas and lead them away from the truth they once held.

Many fearful Christians worry over every meal, every item of clothing, every thought and word, fearing that everything might be sinful when, in reality, it is lawful. They view unavoidable weaknesses as serious sins. All these concerns are groundless troubles and amount to excessive sorrow.

Sorrow is excessive when it overwhelms a person's nature and harms their physical health or understanding. Grace is the proper qualification of nature, and duty is its rightful use; neither should destroy the person. Just as civil, ecclesiastical, and domestic governments exist for edification and not destruction, so self-government should preserve and build up life rather than ruin it.

Jesus said, "I desire mercy and not sacrifice" (Matthew 9:13). He who would not have us harm our neighbor under the guise of religion would not have us harm ourselves, since we are commanded to love our neighbor as ourselves. Fasting, for example, is a duty only so long as it serves a good purpose—expressing true humility or subduing some fleshly desire. So it is with sorrow for sin: it becomes excessive when it does more harm than good. More on this will follow.

1. When Sorrow Is Excessive

When sorrow consumes a sinner it becomes excessive and must be restrained. The passions of grief and mental turmoil often disrupt clear, rational use of reason, corrupting and distorting judgment. In such states judgment cannot be trusted.

Just as a person in a fit of rage misperceives things, so someone in fear or great distress does not see things as they truly are but only as their emotions portray them — whether about God, religion, their own soul and actions, or their friends and enemies. Their judgment is distorted and often incorrect. Like an inflamed eye, everything appears tainted by their sorrow. When sorrow so distorts reason, it is excessive.

Excessive sorrow prevents a person from managing their thoughts. Ungoverned thoughts are both sinful and deeply troubling. Grief sweeps them away like a torrent.

It is almost as difficult to keep the leaves of trees still and orderly in a strong wind as to control the thoughts of someone overwhelmed by distressing emotions. If reason attempts to redirect their mind to more positive or uplifting subjects, it finds itself powerless against the current of passion.

Excessive sorrow can even consume faith itself and greatly hinder its exercise. The gospel invites us to believe in things of unspeakable joy. But a grieving, troubled soul finds it nearly impossible to trust in anything joyful—especially the immense joy of pardon and salvation.

Such people may not lie to God, yet they struggle to accept His free and full promises and His readiness to welcome penitent, returning sinners. Intense grief produces feelings that contradict the grace and promises of the gospel and so obstruct true faith.

Excessive sorrow also attacks hope, particularly when people accept God's word as true for others but cannot believe its promises apply to themselves. Hope is the grace by which a soul, having believed the gospel, confidently expects that its promised benefits will be theirs.

The first act of faith acknowledges the truth of the gospel and its offer of grace and glory through Christ. The next act commits the soul to Christ, accepting Him as Savior and refuge. Then hope declares that this salvation will be theirs. Yet melancholy—overwhelming sorrow and distress—is as hostile to hope as water is to fire. Despair is its very essence.

Those under its power would gladly embrace hope, but it remains elusive. Their thoughts fill with suspicion and doubt; they see only danger and misery and feel utterly helpless. When hope, the anchor of the soul, is lost, it is no surprise they are constantly tossed about by storms.

Excessive sorrow extinguishes any comforting sense of God's infinite goodness and love, making it hard for the soul to love Him. In this it opposes the very essence of holiness.

A troubled soul finds it exceedingly difficult even to grasp God's goodness, and harder still to believe He is good and loving toward them. They are like a person stranded in the Libyan desert, scorched by the sun and dying of thirst. Such a one may know the sun is vital and a blessing to others, yet to them it feels only like torture and death.

In the same way, these souls may admit God is good to others but see Him as an enemy intent on their ruin. They think He hates them and has abandoned them. How then can they love a God they imagine will condemn them—especially when they suppose He decreed this from eternity and brought them into the world for no other purpose? Loving a perceived enemy is hard enough when that enemy merely slanders or wrongs you; how much harder to love a God thought to condemn without remedy.

Consequently, this disorder becomes a false and harmful judge of all God's words, works, mercies, and corrections. Whatever such a person reads or hears, they interpret as aimed at them. Every solemn word or warning in Scripture seems directed specifically at them.

They feel excluded from the promises and comforts, as if they were explicitly named exceptions. God's mercies are minimized and not recognized as mercies; instead they are seen as tools to magnify sin, increase burden, and deepen condemnation. They imagine God is disguising poison as medicine, acting from hatred rather than love, and intent on plunging them deeper into ruin. If God corrects them, they assume it is merely the start of their suffering, convinced He is tormenting them prematurely.

This shows that sorrow is an enemy to thankfulness. It reproaches God for His mercies and treats them as injuries rather than offering heartfelt gratitude.

This disorder is entirely contrary to the joy of the Holy Spirit and to the peace central to God's kingdom. Nothing appears joyful to such distressed souls.

Finding delight in God, His word, and His ways is the essence and vitality of true religion. Yet those I describe find joy in nothing – neither in God nor in Scripture nor in any duty. They resemble a sick person who eats only out of necessity, doing so with loathing and aversion.

All this demonstrates that the affliction stands opposed to the very nature of the gospel. Christ came to deliver captives, to reconcile sinners to God, and to bring glad tidings of pardon and everlasting joy. Where the gospel is received, it is met with rejoicing, as proclaimed by angels and men.

But under this disorder, all that Christ has done, purchased, offered, and promised becomes a source of doubt and sadness.

This disorder greatly serves Satan, who aims to plant blasphemous ideas about God – portraying Him as malevolent, hateful, and destructive, even toward those who seek to please Him. The devil wants to depict God as like himself: a malicious enemy who delights in harm.

If people rightly despise the devil for his harmfulness, he will work to incite hatred and blasphemy against God by convincing them God is even more harmful. Worshiping God in the form of an image is detestable because it suggests He is like a creature. How much worse, then, to conceive of Him as like malicious devils?

Holding diminished, low thoughts of God's goodness and greatness is a grave sin that deeply offends Him – almost as if you believed He was no better or more trustworthy than a mere father or friend. To think of Him as disordered souls imagine is far worse. You would wrong His ministers if you described them as Christ depicts false prophets – harmful thorns, thistles, and wolves. Is it not far worse to think of God in an even more negative light?

Excessive sorrow makes a person unfit for any profitable meditation. It confuses their thoughts and draws them toward harmful distractions and temptations. The more they ponder, the more they become overwhelmed.

It turns prayer into mere complaints rather than childlike, believing supplications.

It completely incapacitates the soul for God's worship, especially for meaningful participation in the sacraments. It breeds greater fear about unworthy reception, which may only hasten and increase their condemnation (1 Corinthians 11:27). Too often it makes preaching and counsel ineffective; no matter how convincing the message, it either fails to change them or is quickly forgotten.

This disorder makes all sufferings feel heavier, since they fall upon a poor, afflicted soul with no comfort to counterbalance them. It makes death exceedingly terrifying, because they believe death will lead them to hell. Life feels burdensome, and death appears dreadful. They grow weary of living and fear dying.

Thus, excessive sorrow consumes a person entirely.

2. The Causes and Cure of Melancholy

What are its causes and cures?

For many people, the primary cause lies in a disorder, weakness, or illness of the body. Such a condition greatly hinders the soul from experiencing any sense of comfort. When sorrow arises from this natural necessity, it is less sinful and less dangerous to the soul, though it remains troublesome, perhaps even more so.

Three diseases cause excessive sorrow:

The first involves intense pain that the body's natural strength cannot endure. However, because this type of pain is usually short-lived, it is not the main concern here.

The second arises from a naturally passionate temperament combined with a weakness in the reasoning powers that should calm that passion. This often appears in elderly people who are greatly weakened and easily offended or angered. Children, likewise, cannot help but cry when they are hurt.

This condition is particularly troublesome and harmful for many women (and some men). They are easily disturbed and hard to soothe, with very little control over themselves. Even many who fear God and who are sound in understanding and quick of wit find they have almost no power against troubling emotions — anger, grief, and especially fear.

Their natural temperament can be a major source of sorrow, fear, and dissatisfaction. Even those who are not truly melancholic often have a childish, ailing, and impatient disposition, so they are easily upset, grieved, or frightened by one thing or another. They resemble an aspen leaf, constantly trembling at the slightest breeze.

The wisest and most patient person cannot please or satisfy such individuals. A single word or even a glance can offend them; every sad story, piece of news, or noise can frighten them. Just as children must have everything they cry for before they will be quiet, so it is with too many adults. This is distressing for those around them, and even more so for themselves. It is less uncomfortable to live with someone who is ill in a house of mourning. Yet as long as reason is not entirely overthrown, the situation is not without remedy, nor is it wholly excusable.

Third, when the brain and imagination are disturbed and reason is partly overthrown by the illness called melancholy, the cure becomes even more difficult. Typically it is those with a naturally fearful and passionate temperament — prone to discontent and grief — who fall into madness and melancholy. The combination of temperament and illness only increases their misery.

3. The Signs of Debilitating Melancholy

I have often described the signs of debilitating melancholy. These include a troubled, restless mind that becomes a settled habit; the person sees nothing but fear and distress. Everything they hear or do feeds this state, and danger seems constantly before their eyes.

Everything they read or hear seems to be against them. They find no joy in anything. Fearful dreams disturb their sleep, and restless thoughts keep them awake. They are offended by others' laughter or happiness. They imagine even a beggar is better off than they are.

They struggle to believe anyone else shares their plight, even when two or three people come to me in the same condition within a week or a day. The similarity is so striking you would think it was the same person's experience being expressed. They take no pleasure in relationships, friends, possessions, or anything else. They feel abandoned by God, convinced that the day of grace is past and that no hope remains for them.

They say they cannot pray except to weep and groan, convinced God will not hear them. They doubt their own sincerity and grace, insist they cannot repent or believe, and feel their hearts utterly hardened.

Often they fear they have committed blasphemy against the Holy Spirit. In sum, fears, troubles, and near despair are their constant state of mind.

If you succeed in showing them they have some evidence of sincerity and that their fears are unfounded and harmful to themselves and to God, they have no counterargument. Yet this realization either relieves none of their distress or the distress returns the next day. The underlying cause remains their physical illness.

You may calm them a hundred times, yet their fears will return a hundred times.

Their misery is that their thoughts are uncontrollable. Trying to persuade them to stop shaking from a fever or to ignore their pain is as futile as persuading them to rid themselves of the self-troubling thoughts or of the overwhelming, confusing ideas that plague them.

They cannot escape these thoughts, day or night. If you tell them to refrain from long, disturbing musings, they cannot comply. If you advise them to cast out false imaginations when Satan introduces them, and to turn their minds elsewhere, they cannot do it. Their thoughts, troubles, and fears are beyond their control, and this lack of control grows worse as their melancholy and madness deepen.

At that stage they often feel something speaking within them, urging them to do this or that. They will recount what it says and when it spoke. They find it hard to believe how much of this is a product of their own imagination.

In this condition they are very ready to believe they have received revelations. Whatever enters their minds they assume is a revelation. They may say that at one time a particular Scripture was placed on their mind and at another time a different one. Often they interpret these texts incorrectly or misapply them to themselves.

They may even apply several texts to reach contradictory conclusions, as if one offers them hope while another seems to contradict it.

As a result, some become very inclined to prophecy, sincerely believing that God has foretold something until it fails to come to pass, and then they feel ashamed. Many turn heretical and adopt erroneous beliefs, truly convinced that God has influenced their thoughts.

Some who have long been troubled find peace and joy by changing their opinions, believing they are now in God's will when before they were not, and that this explained their prior lack of comfort. I have known people who found solace by embracing completely opposite beliefs. Some have converted to Catholicism and to superstition, while others have turned away from Catholicism. Some have found comfort by becoming Anabaptists, others Antinomians, others Arminians, others perfectionists, and still others Quakers.

Others turn away from Christianity altogether, embracing infidelity, denying the afterlife, and living in immoral indulgence. These melancholic heretics and apostates commonly cast off their sadness by such changes. I will not address those people further.

The more sorrowful and sincere, feeling this internal turmoil, often become convinced they are possessed by the devil or at least bewitched. I will say more about this shortly.

Many are tormented by blasphemous thoughts; they tremble at them yet cannot keep them out of their minds. They are tempted and haunted by doubts about Scripture, Christianity, or the afterlife, or by negative thoughts about God.

Often, they feel an internal compulsion, as if something within them urges them to utter blasphemous words about God or to renounce Him. They tremble at these suggestions, yet they persist; some unfortunate souls succumb to this temptation and speak ill of God. Immediately after doing so, something within them declares, "Now, your damnation is sealed; you have sinned against the Holy Spirit; there is no hope." When it escalates too far, they may feel compelled to impose vows upon themselves, such as never speaking again or refusing to eat; some have even starved themselves to death.

When the situation becomes extreme, they often believe they are seeing apparitions. They report various likenesses, especially lights at night around their beds. Sometimes they are convinced they hear voices or feel something touching or hurting them.

They withdraw from company and can do nothing but sit alone and reflect.

They abandon all responsibilities and refuse to engage in the diligent work required by their vocations.

When their condition becomes severe, they grow weary of life and are plagued by temptations to end their existence. It is as if something within urges them to drown themselves, cut their own throats, hang themselves, or throw themselves from a height — which, unfortunately, many have done.

If they manage to escape all of this, when the illness reaches its peak they become completely agitated.

These are the sorrowful symptoms and effects of melancholy. Therefore it is very important to prevent them or to seek a cure while they are just beginning, before they develop into a more serious condition.

4. Possession by the Devil

Here I must address whether such individuals are possessed by the devil, and how much of what has been described can be attributed to him.

I must tell the sincere, melancholy person that understanding the devil's influence in their situation can bring more comfort than despair.

First, we must clarify what is meant by Satan's possession, whether of the body or the soul. It is not merely his physical presence within a person that constitutes possession; we know little about how much more he may be present with a wicked person than with a righteous one. Rather, Satan's possession involves exerting power over a person through a specific, effective operation.

The Spirit of God is present even with the worst individuals, prompting many holy thoughts in the souls of the unrepentant. He is also a consistent and powerful influence within the soul of a believer; thus He is said to dwell in believers and to possess them through habits of holiness and love. In contrast, while Satan frequently attempts to influence the faithful, he truly possesses the souls of the ungodly only by establishing dominant habits of unbelief and sensuality.

Moreover, God permits Satan to inflict persecution, hardships, and ordinary illnesses on the righteous. But when he acts as God's executioner, inflicting extraordinary afflictions—especially on the mind, depriving people of reason and understanding, and operating beyond the natural course of the illness—this is what is called possession.

Just as many evil thoughts in the soul have Satan as their origin while our own hearts supply a source, so many physical illnesses are permitted by God through Satan, though there are also causes within the body itself. Our own failings, moods, the season, the weather, and accidents can be causes. Still, Satan may act more powerfully through these means.

When his actions are such that we label them possession, he may nevertheless operate through natural means and physical conditions. Sometimes he acts in ways that surpass the power of the illness itself—when the uneducated speak in unfamiliar languages, or when bewitched people vomit objects like iron or glass. At other times, he operates solely through the illness itself, as in cases of epilepsy or madness.

From all this, it is easy to conclude that:

1. For Satan to possess the body is not a definitive sign of being graceless, nor does it condemn the soul of anyone unless the soul itself is possessed. In fact, few of God's children are likely never to be occasionally afflicted by Satan acting as God's instrument of correction or trial, as in the case of Job. Contrary to what some claim, it is probable that "a thorn in the flesh"—Satan's messenger to torment Paul—was a physical pain, perhaps an undischarged kidney stone. After praying three times, Paul received only the promise that God's grace would be sufficient for him. (2 Corinthians 12:7-9)

3. No sin indicates Satan's damnable possession of a person except the sin the individual loves more than they hate it—one they would rather keep than abandon and to which they willfully cling.

4. This is a great comfort for those melancholy, honest souls, if they have the understanding to accept it: among all people, none despises their sin more than they do. Indeed, it is the heavy burden of their souls. Do you love your unbelief, your fears, your distracting thoughts, and your temptations to blasphemy? Would you rather keep them than be freed from them? The proud, the ambitious, the fornicators, the drunkards, the gamblers, and the idle who waste time on games and frivolous talk—all of these love their sins and would not abandon them.

Just as Esau sold his birthright for a single meal, such people would risk losing God, Christ, their souls, and heaven rather than give up a sinful habit. But is this your situation? Do you truly love your sorrowful condition? You are weary and burdened, and therefore you are invited to come to Me for rest. (Matthew 11:28-29)

5. Furthermore, it is the devil's strategy to torment those he cannot overcome with enticing, destructive temptations by assaulting them with troubling temptations. He stirs up storms of persecution from without as soon as they begin to escape his deceptions. He also troubles them from within, as far as God allows. We do not deny that Satan plays a significant role in the struggles of such melancholy individuals, since his temptations often lead to the sins for which God corrects them.

His actions often cause bodily disorder.

As a tempter, he is responsible for the sinful and troubling thoughts, doubts, fears, and passions that arise from melancholy.

The devil cannot do whatever he wants with us; he can act only on what we allow him to. He cannot force his way into our lives, but he can enter if we leave the door open. He easily tempts a sluggish, phlegmatic person to laziness, a weak, choleric one to anger, a strong, sanguine one to lust, someone with a strong appetite to gluttony or drunkenness, and vain, playful youth to idleness, gambling, and indulgence— temptations that would have little effect on others. Thus, if he can lead you into melancholy, he can readily tempt you to excessive sorrow and fear, distracting doubts and thoughts, murmuring against God, despair, and even blasphemous thoughts about God. If he does not use that route, he may lead you into fanatical ideas of revelation and a prophesying spirit.

I would add that God will not hold you accountable for Satan's mere temptations, however severe, provided you do not willingly accept them but hate them. Nor will He condemn you for the harmful effects that are unavoidable due to the power of a physical illness—just as He would not condemn someone for irrational thoughts or words during a fever, frenzy, or complete madness. However, when reason still has some influence and the will can control the passions, you are responsible if you do not use that power. The difficulty lessens the fault, but does not remove it.

5. Other Usual Causes

There are usually other causes that precede this melancholy, except in some who are naturally predisposed. Before discussing its cure, I will briefly touch on these causes.

One of the most common causes is sinful impatience, discontent, and worry. These spring from a sinful attachment to some bodily interest, a failure to submit sufficiently to God's will, and a lack of trust in Him. They also arise from not considering heaven a satisfying reward. I use all these terms to convey the true nature of this complex disease of the soul. The names show it is a combination of many sins, each of which is serious. If these sins were the prevailing inclination and habit of one's heart and life, they would indicate a graceless state. However, as long as they are hated and do not outweigh grace, and our heavenly inheritance is valued, chosen, and sought more than earthly prosperity, God's mercy through Christ forgives them and will ultimately deliver us from them all. Still, it is fitting for even a forgiven sinner to understand the seriousness of these sins so they do not treat them lightly or become ungrateful for forgiveness. Therefore, I will clearly outline the aspects of this sin that lead many into deep melancholy.

We assume God tests His servants in this life with various afflictions, and Christ calls us to deny ourselves, take up our cross, and follow Him with submissive patience. Some are tested with painful illnesses; others with wrongs from enemies, unkindness from friends, difficult or provoking relatives and associates, slander, persecution, and many with losses, disappointments, or poverty.

Here, impatience is the starting point of this sinful malady. Our natures often focus too much on the interests of the flesh and are too weak to bear heavy burdens. Poverty brings trials that those who are well-off and do not experience them tend to overlook. This is particularly evident in two situations:

1. When individuals have not only themselves to care for but also a wife and children in need.

2. When they are indebted to others. This is a heavy burden for an honest conscience, though dishonest borrowers may take it lightly.

In times of hardship and trial, people tend to become overly sensitive and impatient. When they and their families lack food, clothing, warmth, and other basic necessities and do not know how to obtain them — when landlords, butchers, bakers, and other creditors demand payment and they cannot pay — it's hard to keep these worries from weighing heavily on the heart. It is especially difficult for women, who may be more prone to excessive emotions. Such impatience can produce a persistent discontent and unrest of spirit that affects the body and becomes a constant burden on the heart.

Impatience and discontent torment the mind with grief and constant worries about how to relieve the situation; those afflicted can think of little else. These anxieties consume the heart much as a fever consumes the body.

The root of all this is a great sin: an excessive love of the body and of this world. If we did not love anything excessively, it would not have power to torment us. If we did not overly cherish ease and health, pain and sickness would be more bearable. If we did not love our children and friends immoderately, their deaths would not overwhelm us with intolerable sorrow. If we did not overvalue our bodies, worldly wealth, and prosperity, we could more easily endure hardship, labor, and want—even the loss of what seems necessary for health and life, if that is God's will. This would spare us many vexations, discontents, cares, excessive grief, and a troubled mind.

There is still more sin at the root of it all. It shows that our wills remain too selfish and are not fully submitted to God's will. Instead, we would be gods to ourselves, choosing and satisfying whatever our flesh desires. We lack a proper resignation of ourselves and all our concerns to God. We do not live as children depending on Him for our daily bread, but feel we must provide for ourselves.

While this may sound sexist to modern ears, women are indeed more susceptible to depression than men. Consider the menstrual cycle, postpartum blues, and menopause. Consider the burdens of childcare, often made worse by an absent, lazy, or unsympathetic husband. Also remember the age in which this was written and the political, social, and financial situations women faced. Such dependency and exclusion took their toll.

This indicates that we are not sufficiently humbled by our sin. If we were, we would be thankful even for our lowest state, recognizing it as far better than what we truly deserve.

There is also a deep distrust of God and unbelief revealed in these discontents and cares. If we could trust God as much as we trust ourselves, or as we trust a faithful friend, or as a child trusts his father, how peaceful would our minds be—knowing His wisdom, all-sufficiency, and love?

Other Usual Causes

This unbelief has an even worse effect than worldly troubles. It shows that people do not regard God's love and the promise of heavenly glory as a sufficient portion unless they also have what they desire for their bodies in this world — freedom from poverty, hardships, provocations, injuries, and pain. All that God has promised them here or in the afterlife, even everlasting glory, is not enough to satisfy them. When God, Christ, and heaven are not enough to calm a person's mind, they lack faith, hope, and love, which are far more important than food and clothing.

Another great cause of mental turmoil is guilt from some willful sin. When the conscience is convicted but the soul not converted, sin is both loved and feared. God's wrath terrifies them, yet not enough to overcome their sin. Some live in secret fraud and robbery; many indulge in drunkenness and secret lusts, whether through self-pollution or fornication. They know that the wrath of God is coming upon the sons of disobedience for such actions. Yet the rage of appetite and lust prevails. They despair and persist in sin; while sparks of hell fall on their consciences, this changes neither their hearts nor their lives.

Even so, there is more hope for recovery for these individuals than for those who are dead-hearted or unbelieving sinners, who, being past feeling, have given themselves over to lasciviousness, to work all uncleanness with greediness. These people are so callous that they will defend their sins and argue against holy obedience to God. Brutishness is not as bad as diabolism and malignity. However, none of these are the individuals referred to in my text. Their sorrow is not excessive, but rather too little — so long as it does not restrain them from their sin.

If God converts these individuals, the sins in which they now live may, upon sober reflection, plunge their souls into depths of sorrow that overwhelm them. When people are truly converted yet continue to flirt with temptation and renew the wounds of conscience by lapses, it is no surprise that their sorrow and fears return. Grievous sins have bound many consciences so tightly that people have been cast into incurable melancholy and distraction.

6. Melancholy and Sin for Christians

Among those who fear God there is another cause of melancholy and excessive sorrow: ignorance and misunderstandings about their peace and comfort. I will outline some specifics.

One issue is ignorance of the essence of the gospel or the covenant of grace, as some libertines (known as Antinomians) dangerously misinterpret it. They claim that Christ has repented and believed on behalf of others, so individuals need not examine their own faith and repentance any more than they would question the righteousness of Christ. Similarly, many well-meaning Christians fail to understand that the gospel is a message of unspeakable joy for all who believe. They do not realize that Christ and life are offered freely to those who accept Him, and that no sins, however many or great, are excluded from pardon for a soul that sincerely turns to God in faith through Christ. They do not see that whoever desires may freely take the water of life, and that all who are weary and heavy laden are invited to come to Him for rest.

They also misunderstand the condition of forgiveness, which is simply genuine consent to the pardoning and saving covenant. Many are confused about the purpose of sorrow for sin and about what a hardened heart really is. They suppose that if their sorrow is not intense enough to bring tears or great distress, they are not fit for pardon — even when they assent to the whole pardoning covenant. They fail to see that God does not desire sorrow for its own sake but the humility that springs from a true sense of sin, danger, and misery. That humility should make us feel our need of Christ and mercy, and should bring us sincerely to consent to be His disciples and to be saved on His covenant terms. Whether sorrow is large or small, if it effects this result, the sinner shall be saved.

Regarding the duration of godly sorrow, some think the pains of the new birth must last a long time. Scripture shows, however, that the gospel has often been received quickly and joyfully by penitent sinners, for it is a gift from Christ along with pardon and everlasting life. Humility and hatred of sin should continue and increase, but our first sorrows may soon be overshadowed by holy thankfulness and joy.

In Scripture, hardness of heart means a stubborn, rebellious obstinacy that prevents a person from being moved from sin to obedience by any of God's commands or threats. It is described as having an iron sinew — or a stiff neck. But it is never defined merely by the absence of tears or of passionate sorrow in someone who is willing to obey. The hardhearted are the truly rebellious. Sorrow, even for sin, can be excessive: a passionate person may weep over sins they refuse to abandon. But obedience cannot be excessive.

Many are discouraged by ignorance of themselves and fail to recognize the sincerity God has granted them. Grace is weak in all of us. Small and weak grace is not easily seen, because it acts faintly and inconsistently and is known chiefly by its acts. Weak grace is always accompanied by strong corruption. All sin in heart and life contradicts and obscures grace. Such people often lack knowledge of their own hearts, and so cannot easily keep firm assurance of their sincerity. If they do gain some assurance with great effort, then neglect of duty, coldness, yielding to temptation, or inconsistency of obedience will make them question it again. A sad, melancholy mind is always apt to conclude the worst and can hardly see anything good or comforting.

In such cases, few know how to draw comfort from mere probabilities when certainty is unattainable. They struggle even more to find comfort in the mere offers of grace and salvation, even when they are willing to accept them. If comfort were only for those with full assurance, despair would swallow up the souls of most true believers.

Ignorance of others can magnify some people's fears and sorrows. They may assume, from our preaching and writing, that pastors are far better than they are. As a result, they may feel graceless because they fall short of those supposed standards. If they lived with us, saw our failings, knew us as well as we know ourselves, or could read our sinful thoughts and vices written on our foreheads, that misconception would be cured.

Unskilled teachers add to many people's grief and confusion. Some cannot clearly explain the covenant of grace. Others lack any experience of spiritual, heavenly consolation. Many have never known inward holiness or renewal by the Holy Spirit. They do not understand what sincerity is or how a saint differs from an ungodly person. Deceivers misrepresent good and evil, sometimes portraying the best as the worst. Some unskilled people place sincerity in mere external duties, as papists do with inventions and superstitions, and as many sects do with their unsound opinions.

Some describe the state of grace inaccurately and dangerously. They outline how far a hypocrite may go, which needlessly discourages and confounds weaker Christians who cannot correct those misrepresentations from their books or teachers. Too many teachers place people's comfort, and sometimes their idea of salvation, on controversies beyond their understanding. They pronounce heresy and damnation on things they do not comprehend. Over the past twelve or thirteen hundred years, the Christian world has been divided by unskillful quarrels about words taken in different senses. Is it any wonder hearers of such teachings are left confused?

I have outlined the causes of distracted sorrows. Now I will discuss their cure. Alas, it is easier said than done. I will begin where the disease starts and explain what the patient must do, and what friends and teachers must do for them.

First, do not view the sinful causes of your troubles as either greater or lesser than they really are.

Too many people in suffering convince themselves they only deserve pity, ignoring the sin that caused their troubles or that they continue to commit. Many unskilled friends and ministers offer comfort when a plain rebuke and exposure of sin would be a more effective part of the cure. If sufferers were more aware of the extent of their sin — overvaluing the world, failing to trust God, thinking harshly of Him, holding shallow and unholy views of His goodness, undervaluing the heavenly glory that should satisfy them even in affliction, and showing daily impatience, anxieties, and discontent — they would find that awareness more healing than mere consoling words. When they say, as Jonah did, "It is right for me to be angry,"

and then treat their denials of grace, distracting sorrows, and complaints against God's love and mercy as if they were duties, it is time to help them see how great a sinner they truly are.

On the other hand, when people foolishly believe that every sin proves they are wholly without grace, and that God will blame them for the devil's temptations — condemning them for what they hate and treating their melancholy as a crime — this error must be corrected and condemned. They should not feed their passions or distress with such falsehoods.

Secondly, do not fall into a habit of irritability and impatience. The chief sin is to love something carnal more than God and His glory, but impatience is not the same as ignorance. Did you not expect to face suffering and to bear your cross when you first committed yourselves to Christ? Do you now find it strange? As 1 Peter 4:12 puts it, do not think it strange concerning the fiery trial which is to try you. Make it a daily practice to prepare for whatever challenges God may bring, so they will not catch you off guard or overwhelm you.

Prepare for the loss of children and friends, for the loss of possessions, and for poverty and need. Prepare for slanders, injuries, or poisoning, for sickness, pain, and death. It is your lack of preparation that makes these experiences seem unbearable.

Remember that it is only the vile body that suffers — a body you always knew would face death and return to dust. Whoever causes your suffering, God uses it to test you. If you think you are merely angry with people, you are still murmuring against God; otherwise His hand would lead you to patient acceptance.

Be especially on guard against a persistent discontent of mind. Do you not already have far more than you deserve? Have you forgotten how many years of undeserved mercy you have enjoyed? Discontent is a continual resistance to God's will, and it does not hesitate to express open rebellion. Your own will rises against His. It is almost atheistic to suppose your sufferings lie outside His providence, yet you still complain against God. Who else has the right to govern you and the whole world?

When you feel anxious about your deliverance, remember that such anxiety is not trusting God. Attend to your own duties and obey His commands, but leave the outcome to Him. Worrying only adds to your afflictions. It is a great mercy from God that He forbids such anxieties and promises to care for you Himself. Your Savior has gently yet firmly admonished you about how sinful and unproductive these worries are, reminding you that your heavenly Father knows that you need all these things (Matthew 6:25-34). If He withholds something from you, it is for a good reason; and if it is to correct you, it is still for your good. If you submit to Him and accept His gifts, He will give you far better than what He takes away — even Christ and eternal life.

Thirdly, set yourselves more diligently than ever to overcome an excessive love of the world. Your troubles can do you much good if you trace them back to their source and discover what you cannot bear to lose or be without. That will reveal what you over-love. God is jealous, even in His love, against every idol loved too much and against any affection that should be His alone. If He removes those idols and tears them from our hands and hearts, that is both merciful and just.

I do not mean those who are troubled only by a lack of faith, holiness, communion with God, or assurance of salvation. Such troubles could give them much comfort if they understood their origin and meaning. Just as impatient distress under worldly hardships shows one loves the world too much, so impatient distress over a lack of holiness and communion with God shows that such believers love holiness and God.

Love precedes desire and sorrow. People delight in what they love while they have it; they grieve its absence and long to possess it. The will is love embodied — no one is troubled by the lack of what they do not desire.

The most common source of intense melancholy often begins with worldly discontent and worry — whether from want, hardship, fear of suffering, provocations by someone close, or a sense of disgrace or contempt. These things breed passionate discontent, and a self-willed person cannot accept the denial of what he desires. Once discontent has clouded and afflicted the mind, temptations against the soul follow.

What began as worldly trouble soon appears to be a matter of religion, conscience, or even the supposed sin of lacking grace.

Why could you not patiently endure the words, wrongs, losses, and hardships that befell you? Why did you make so much of these temporary, bodily matters? Is it not because you loved them too much? Were you not sincere when you called them vanity and promised to leave them in God's hands? Would you have God leave you in so great a sin as the love of the world, or let what is due to Him be given to mere creatures? If God does not teach you what to love and what to despise, and cure you of the dangerous disease of a worldly spirit, He will not fit you for holiness or prepare you for heaven.

Souls do not rise to heaven against their will, like an arrow shot upward; rather they rise like a fire that naturally ascends while earthly things drag them down. When holy people die, their souls incline upward by a natural tendency; their love gives that inclination. They love God, heaven, holy company, godly friends, and righteous deeds, including mutual affection and joyful praise of God. This spirit and love are like a fiery nature that carries them toward heaven. Angels do not force them there but guide them, like a bride led to her wedding, carried all the way by love.

Conversely, the souls of the wicked are drawn toward the flesh and the world. They do not love heavenly deeds or company, and have nothing within to attract them to God. Instead they love worldly trinkets and sensual pleasures, even if they cannot enjoy them — as the poor long for riches and are vexed by their lack. Therefore it is no wonder that wicked souls dwell with devils in the lower regions and sometimes appear here when God permits — nor is it surprising that holy souls are not subject to such decline. Love is the soul's balance and spring, drawing souls either downward or upward.

Therefore, cast aside earthly, fleshly love. How long will you remain here, and what can earth and flesh do for you? God will not deny what assists you in holiness and prepares you for heaven, if you are submissive. But to love created things too much is to turn away from God; it is a dangerous disease of the soul that drags it down from heaven. Had you learned to forsake everything for Christ and to regard all as loss and refuse, as Paul said (Philippians 3:8), you would more easily endure their absence.

When have you seen anyone live in discontent and be tormented by melancholy, grief, and worry over the lack of refuse, a bubble, a shadow, or a fleeting dream? If you will not learn otherwise, God will teach you by sorrow.

Fourthly, if you are not convinced that God alone, Christ alone, and heaven alone are sufficient for your happiness and complete contentment, then go and study this matter further; you may be persuaded. Learn your catechism and the principles of religion. Then you will know how to lay up treasures in heaven rather than on earth, and you will see that to be with Christ is best.

Death destroys all worldly glory and levels the rich and poor; it is the common gateway to heaven or hell. Your conscience will not ask whether you lived in pleasure or pain, in wealth or in poverty, but whether you lived for God or for the flesh; whether you lived for heaven or for earth. What took precedence in your heart and life? If there is shame in heaven, you will feel ashamed there for having complained and grumbled about lacking what the flesh desired on earth, and for arriving there grieving because your body suffered here. Strive to live by faith, hoping in the unseen promised glory with Christ, and you will endure any suffering on the way.

Fifthly, study how great a sin it is to set your own will and desires against the wisdom, will, and providence of God, making your will a god in His place. Does not a murmuring heart secretly accuse God? Every such accusation against God has some degree of blasphemy, for the murmurer implies that something about God is blameworthy. If you dare not openly accuse Him, do not let the murmurs of your heart do so. Much of religion and holiness consists in bringing this rebellious self-will to full resignation, submission, and alignment with God's will. Until you can find rest in God's will, you will never know true rest.

Sixthly, study how essential it is to trust God and our blessed Redeemer fully with your soul, your body, and all you possess. Is it not reasonable to trust infinite power, wisdom, and goodness? Is it not fitting to trust a Savior who came from heaven in the flesh and saved sinners by such incomprehensible acts of love? Who else will you trust — yourselves or your friends? Who has sustained you all your life and accomplished all that has been done for you? Who has saved the souls now in heaven? What is our Christianity if not a life of faith?

Is your faith to be consumed by worries and troubles if God does not shape every providence to your desires? Seek first the kingdom of God and His righteousness, and all these things shall be added to you (Matthew 6:33). He has said that not a hair of your head shall be lost (Luke 21:18), for they are all numbered. Not one sparrow falls to the ground apart from your Father's will (Matthew 10:29). Does He care less for those who desire to please Him? Trust God, and your cares, fears, and grief will diminish.

Oh, if only you understood what a mercy and comfort it is that God makes it your duty to trust Him! If He had made no promises, the command itself would be as good as a promise. If He simply commands you to trust Him, you may be sure He will not betray your trust. If a faithful and capable friend asks you to trust him for relief, you would not doubt that he would not deceive you.

I have friends who would trust me with their estates, lives, and souls if it were in my power, and they would not fear that I would harm them. Yet they cannot trust the God of infinite goodness with these matters, even though He commands them to trust Him and has promised that He will never leave them nor forsake them. That refuge calms my fears — that God, my Father and Redeemer, has commanded me to trust Him with my body, health, liberty, and possessions. When eternity seems strange and frightening, He invites me to trust Him with my departing soul. Heaven and earth are upheld by Him; how can I distrust Him?

Objection: But only His children will He save.

Response: True. All are His children who genuinely desire to obey and please Him. If you truly will be holy and follow His commands in a godly, righteous, and sober way, you may confidently rest in His will. Rejoice in His acceptance and rewards, for He will forgive all our weaknesses through the merits and intercession of Christ.

Seventhly, if you do not want to be overwhelmed by sorrow, avoid the temptations of sinful pleasure. Passions, dullness, and neglected duties carry various degrees of guilt. But the enjoyment of sin is the most dangerous and deeply wounding. Flee the temptations of lust, pride, ambition, greed, and an uncontrolled appetite for food or drink, just as you would flee from guilt, grief, and fear. The more pleasure you take in sin, the more sorrow it will ultimately bring.

Moreover, the more you know something is sin, and your conscience tells you that God opposes it, yet you continue and suppress your conscience, the more it will torment you later. It will be harder to quiet when it is awakened to repentance.

Indeed, when a humbled soul is forgiven by grace and believes he is forgiven, he will still struggle to forgive himself. Memories of willful sin, how slight the temptation was, and the mercies and motives he ignored will make him displeased and angry with himself. He may loathe his own wickedness, which will hinder a swift or easy reconciliation. When we remember that we sinned knowingly—even while aware that God sees us and that we have offended Him—doubts about our sincerity will linger. We will fear that we still have the same heart and would commit the same sins if faced with the same temptations.

Do not expect joy or peace while you live in willful, cherished sin. That thorn must be removed from your heart before you can be relieved of the pain—unless God leaves you with a hardened heart and Satan gives you a deceptive peace that only prepares you for greater sorrow.

Eighthly, if none of the sins already mentioned are the source of your sorrows, but your troubles arise from confused thoughts about religion or the state of your soul—such as fearing God's wrath for past sins, or doubting your sincerity and salvation—then the previous admonitions do not apply. Instead, I will offer the appropriate remedy: cure the ignorance and errors that cause your distress.

Many are troubled by doctrinal controversies. Each opposing faction is confident and has much to say, and their words may seem true to the uninformed and hard for a listener to refute. Each party claims its way is the only way and threatens damnation to those who do not convert. The Catholics assert, "There is no salvation outside our church," meaning only subjects of the Bishop of Rome are saved. The Orthodox condemn the Catholics and exalt their own church, as does every faction. Some would force conversion by fire and sword, declaring, "Join our church, or face imprisonment," while others create a prison within their church by excluding the incapable and unwilling.

Question: Among all these, how shall the ignorant know what to choose?

Answer: The situation is unfortunate, yet not as dire as that of the vast majority of the world, who are immersed in heathenism or disbelief or who do not concern themselves with religion at all. They merely follow the customs of their countries and the laws of their rulers to avoid suffering.

It is a sign of your regard for God and your salvation that you are troubled about religion and eager to know which is right. Even engaging in controversy is better than being indifferent to atheism, provided you stand on the right side, whatever that may be. If you throw acorns or seeds among swine, they will fight over them; if it is carrion, dogs will contend for it. But if it is gold or jewels, dogs and swine will not fight over them; they will only trample them into the dirt. When these treasures are presented to men, they will grab each other by the ears to obtain them. Lawyers argue about the law, princes about power, and others pay no attention. Religious people debate religion; what is surprising about that? It shows they value their souls and their faith, even if their understanding is still imperfect. If you follow the straightforward guidelines below, controversies need not disturb your peace.

7. Guidelines for Peace

Regarding God's NATURAL REVELATION, adhere to the light and law of nature, which all people are obliged to observe. Even apart from Scripture or Christianity, the works of God (nature) show us that God exists (Romans 1:20) and that He rewards those who diligently seek Him (Hebrews 11:6).

They reveal that God is absolutely perfect in power, knowledge, and goodness, and that man is a rational, free agent created by Him. Therefore humanity belongs to God and is under His will and governance. Nature indicates that human actions are not arbitrary: some things we ought to do, and some we ought not to do — virtue and vice, moral good and evil, are plainly different.

Thus there is a universal law that obliges us to do good and forbids us from doing evil; this law can only be the law of the universal governor, who is God. It tells all people that they owe God absolute obedience because He is their most wise and sovereign ruler, and that they owe Him their highest love, since He is not only our chief benefactor but also perfectly admirable in Himself. It shows that He has made us sociable members of one world, and that we owe love and assistance to one another.

It assures us that obedience to God can never be in vain or detrimental to us. It also reminds us that we all must die, and that earthly pleasures and this fleeting world will soon abandon us. There is no more reason to doubt any of this than to doubt that man is man. Be true to this much, and it will greatly assist you in everything else.

As for God's SUPERNATURAL REVELATION, hold fast to God's Word, the Holy Bible. It was written under the special inspiration of the Holy Spirit and is a sufficient record of that revelation.

It is not divine faith if it does not rest on divine revelation, nor is obedience truly divine if it does not submit to divine governance and command. A man's word should be believed only to the extent that it deserves human faith. Likewise, a man's law must be obeyed according to the measure of his authority. These human faiths and obediences are far removed from the divine.

There is no universal ruler of the world or the church except God; no man, nor any council of men, is capable of that office. God's law exists in nature and in the Holy Scripture. That law will be the standard by which He judges us, and thus the only divine rule for our faith, judgment, hearts, and lives. While not everything in Scripture is equally clear or necessary, a person may still be saved without understanding many passages, for all that is essential for salvation is plainly contained there. God's law is perfect for its intended purpose; it requires no supplement from man.

Hold firmly to the sufficiency of Scripture, or you will never know what to believe. Councils and canons are far more uncertain; there is no consensus among their makers about which rulings are obligatory and which are not, nor any feasible way to reach agreement.

Yet use the assistance of others with gratitude in understanding and obeying the Word of God.

Guidelines for Peace

Although lawyers, in their official capacity, do not possess legislative power, you need their help to apply the law correctly. And although no individuals have authority to make laws for the universal church, we must rely on teachers to understand and apply God's laws.

We are not born with faith or knowledge; apart from what our senses perceive or what reason deduces, we know nothing except what is taught to us. If you ask, "From whom must we learn?" I answer, "From those who know and have learned themselves." No name, title, relationship, or habit can enable anyone to teach you what they do not themselves know.

1. Children must learn from their parents and tutors.

2. People must learn from their capable and faithful pastors and catechizers.

3. All Christians must be teachers by providing charitable assistance to one another.

However, teaching and law-making are distinct activities. To teach another is simply to show them the same evidence of truth by which the teacher knows it, so that the learner may understand it as well. To say, "You must believe that what I say is true, and that this is its meaning," is not teaching but law-giving. Believing such a person is not the same as learning or knowing, though some degree of human faith in our teachers is necessary for learners.

Do not accept anything as necessary for Christianity and salvation that is not recorded in Scripture and that has not been held necessary by true Christians in every age and place. This does not mean we must first prove a man to be a true Christian before we may learn Christian truth from him. Plain Scripture tells all people what Christianity is, and by Scripture we discern whom to recognize as Christians.

If something is new and has arisen since the apostles wrote Scripture, it cannot be an essential part of Christianity. Otherwise Christianity would be changeable, and it would not be the same now as before; or there would have been no Christians before the novelty. The church would not be the church, nor any individual a Christian, if they lacked any essential component of faith or practice.

But be wary of the deceit of sophists. Although nothing is necessary for salvation except what all sound Christians have consistently believed, it does not follow that everything believed or practiced by many good Christians is therefore true, good, or valid — much less the opinions held by the more tempted among them.

The essence of Christianity has always been the same, yet Christians' opinions, mistakes, and faults are not part of that essential faith. Human nature is fundamentally the same in Adam and in all men; but the diseases of nature are another matter. If all men fall into sin and error, so do all churches. Their Christianity comes from God; their corruptions and maladies do not.

Hold to nothing except what Christians of old received from God's Word. But because they all have faults and errors, you must not adopt or practice all that they have believed or done.

Endeavoring to keep the unity of the Spirit in the bond of peace, live in love within the communion of saints — that is, with those who believe in and obey the Christian faith and law (Ephesians 4:3). You will know them by their fruits (Matthew 7:16).

The societies of malignants — those who suppress true practical knowledge and piety, who hate the best people, and who foster wickedness while cruelly persecuting those who, in conscience, refuse their usurpations and inventions — are not the communion of saints. Wolves, thorns, and thistles are not the sheep or vines of Christ.

In your learning or fellowship, do not privilege any peculiar or singular sect above the universal consensus of the faithful, as far as human judgment allows.

Although our faith does not come from the number of believers, and although most are not the best while a few are far wiser than the majority, in a controversy a few knowledgeable persons should be preferred to a multitude with less understanding.

Christ is the head of all true Christians, not merely of a particular sect or party. He has commanded all His people to live as brothers, in love and holy fellowship. In most fields of study, a larger number of agreeing individuals are more likely to be right than a few isolated persons who show no greater ability than the majority. At the very least, even in less essential matters you must preserve unity with all true Christians and avoid unnecessary differences.

Never set a doubtful opinion against a certain truth or duty. Do not turn certain matters into uncertain ones; instead, make uncertain matters certain. For example, it is certain that you should live in love and peace with all true Christians, do good to all, and wrong none. Do not let doubtful differences lead you to violate this rule. Do not hate, slander, backbite, or harm them over an indifferent or unnecessary point.

Do not prefer your mint, anise, and cummin, or your tithes and ceremonies, over justice, mercy, and faith, or set them against the weighty and certain principles of the law (Matthew 23:23). Such a sect or opinion that contradicts the nature and common duties of Christianity and humanity is misguided.

Faithfully serve Christ to the extent you have attained, and be true to all the truth you know. Do not sin by omission or act against the knowledge you possess, lest God, for this reason, send you a strong delusion so that you may believe a lie (2 Thessalonians 2:11).

Remember that all men on earth know only in part. We see as though in a mirror, dimly, and therefore even the best among us are full of errors (1 Corinthians 13:12). No one knows even the smallest blade of grass or the humblest worm with perfect understanding. If God permits many errors in all of us, we must tolerate those that are bearable in one another.

It is commendable to be humble, teachable, and eager to learn. We have seen few as defective as those who claim sinless perfection, and few as fallible as the Roman sect that asserts its infallibility. When they insist you must accept their popes and councils to resolve every controversy, ask whether we can ever expect perfect resolution of ignorance, error, and sin. If not, what hope is there of resolving every controversy before we reach heaven, where ignorance will cease?

The controversies about the essentials of Christianity were settled for us when we became true and mature Christians. The remaining disputes will lessen as we grow in knowledge and, indeed, we are to grow in the grace and knowledge of our Lord and Savior Jesus Christ (2 Peter 3:18). Theology is no less obscure than law or medicine, where controversies abound.

Do not limit yourself in knowledge, or say, "We have learned enough." Continue as Christ's students, learning more and more until death. Even the wisest know little and can still grow.

There is a real difference in usefulness and comfort between those with clear, well-ordered knowledge and those with confused, disorganized ideas.

These rules, when practiced, will save you from being troubled by doubts and controversies raised by religious pretenders.

8. For Those Troubled by Sin

If your troubles are not doctrinal disputes but concern your sins, lack of grace, or spiritual condition, carefully consider the following truths and advice. They will help you find healing.

God's goodness equals His greatness, including the power that rules heaven and earth. His attributes are consistent, and His goodness is given to those who can receive it. He loved us while we were still His enemies, for He is love by nature.

Christ willingly assumed human nature and satisfied the claims of sin for the world. His sacrifice is so sufficient that no one fails for want of merit in Him.

On the basis of His merits, Christ has established a covenant of grace. That covenant pardons sin and freely grants eternal life to all who, by faith, accept it. Thus all sins are forgiven conditionally under its terms.

The condition for pardon and life is not that we sin no more, nor that we can buy it or earn it by works. The sole requirement is faith: that we believe in Him and willingly accept the mercy He freely offers, consistent with the nature of the gift. Practically, this means receiving Christ as Savior—one who justifies, sanctifies, rules over, and saves us.

God has commissioned His ministers to proclaim this covenant of grace to everyone, urgently calling them in His name to accept it and be reconciled. He has excluded no one.

No one who accepts this offer will be condemned; only those who persistently refuse it to the end will face damnation.

The day of grace has not passed for any sinner: anyone may still have Christ and pardon if they desire. If they lack it, it is because they choose not to accept it. Grace remains available and is being actively offered to all who will receive it.

In God's sight the will represents the person. A person's inward disposition determines what they become. Consent to the baptismal covenant is true grace and conversion, giving such persons a right to Christ and to eternal life (John 1:12). The number and greatness of past sins do not exclude any penitent, converted sinner from pardon; God forgives both great and small sins. Where sin abounds, grace abounds much more, and when much is forgiven it produces gratitude and love (Luke 7:47). True repentance may exist without many tears or violent sorrow, provided a person truly desires to leave the sin and not cling to it, and sincerely strives, though imperfectly, to overcome it. No sin will condemn someone who hates it more than they love it and genuinely intends to forsake it, as shown by earnest effort.

Even the best have much evil in them, and even the worst retain some good. What distinguishes the godly from the wicked is which rules the will—the good or the evil. A truly godly person counts God, heaven, and holiness as superior to worldly pleasures and sinful desires, and such a person will be saved.

Even the best among us need pardon every day—even for the faults that appear in their holiest actions. They must rely on Christ each day for forgiveness.

Regenerate people often commit sins against light and conscience. They have more knowledge than others and more sensitive consciences. They would be truly happy if they could be as good as they know they ought to be, if they loved God as they should, and if they were free from the remaining passions and unbelief their conscience calls sinful.

God does not count Satan's temptations as our sins; He holds us responsible only for failing to resist them. Christ Himself was tempted even to the worst sin—to fall down and worship the devil. God will hold Satan accountable for his blasphemous temptations.

The thoughts, fears, and distress produced by melancholy, natural weakness, or bodily disorder are more a matter of physical illness than of sin. They are among the lesser faults—no more sinful than thirst or fever—except insofar as some prior sin produced the disease, or insofar as the person still has the capacity to resist them.

Certainty about our faith and about our sincerity is not required for salvation; genuine sincerity of faith is. One who gives himself to Christ will be saved, even if he doubts the sincerity of that giving. Christ knows His own grace even when those who have it cannot see it. Only a few true Christians attain certainty of salvation; weak grace, weighed down by corruption, is hard to discern and commonly comes with fear and doubt.

A reasonable probability of sincerity and trust in Christ is enough to let a person live and die in peace, even without absolute certainty. Otherwise, almost no Christian would have peace, yet many do.

For about four hundred years after Christ, most church writers taught that those who did not persevere in faith might fall from a state of grace which, had they persevered, would have saved them. Thus only the strong and confirmed could claim certainty. Many Protestant churches still teach this, yet their members do not live in despair.

No one can be sure they will not fall as grievously as David or Peter did. But if there is no good reason to think such a fall likely, one need not live in constant terror. A wife or child cannot be certain their husband or father will never harm them, yet people commonly live without fear.

Even when faith is so weak that we question the gospel or the afterlife, and when trust in Christ does not banish our fears, such faith can still save us if there is sufficient evidence for the gospel and a reasonable hope of a better life to come. That should move us to place our hopes and choices on seeking first the kingdom of God and His righteousness—giving those hopes priority over worldly desires—and to live a holy life to attain it.

God's love and promise in Christ give such a firm foundation for faith and comfort that everyone should trust Him with confidence and peace, and live joyfully in that holy hope.

If you doubt your salvation because of the gravity of your sins, the way to peace is a prompt willingness to forsake them. The complainer must either be resolved to be holy and abandon sin or not. If you refuse to let sin go and instead love and cling to it, why do you complain and grieve over what you cherish? If a child cried about a sour apple but kept eating it, you would not console the child—you would correct the stubbornness. Yet if you truly desire to leave sin, you are already freed from its condemning guilt.

If you doubt the sincerity of your faith and your other graces, and self-examination leaves you uncertain, the quickest way to resolve the doubt is to give yourself to Christ. If you have been unsure whether you were truly a believer, be certain that Christ is now offered to you. If you consent to the covenant and accept that offer, you may be assured that He is yours.

Simply examining yourself is not always the best path to assurance. Instead, strive to awaken and exercise the grace you seek assurance of. Study God's promises and His goodness until active faith confirms your belief. Love God and His glory until you are assured of that love.

Our standing is not proved by some extraordinary act, whether good or bad. It is shown by the predominant inclination, direction, and overall character of your heart and life.

Even when we cry out that we cannot believe, cannot love God, and cannot pray rightly, Christ can help us. Without His grace we can do nothing; yet His grace is sufficient. He does not withhold further help once He has made us willing. He encourages us to ask for it. "If any of you lacks wisdom, let him ask of God, who gives to all liberally and without reproach, and it will be given to him." (James 1:5)

The blasphemy of the Holy Spirit is not the sin of everyone who believes that Jesus is the Christ, nor of everyone who fears it, nor of every unbeliever—but of a few stubborn, unbelieving enemies. It consists in seeing the miracles of Christ and the work of His Spirit that should prove His divinity, and, having no other excuse, calling them the work of a conjurer or of the devil.

Sinful fear is very troubling and should not be indulged, yet God often permits and uses it for good. It keeps us from being bold in sin and from indulging sinful pleasures and the love of the world. It guards us against presumption and complacency, which are far more dangerous. Proper fear also helps to reduce pride and keeps us watchful. It is meant to protect us from the harm we dread.

Those who approach heaven with fear and trembling will soon be free from all fear, doubts, and heaviness forever.

When Christ was in His agony for our sins and cried out, "My God, My God, why have You forsaken Me?" He was still beloved by His Father. He was tempted so that He might help those who are tempted, and He endured derision to become a compassionate High Priest to those who suffer. (Hebrews 4:15) The more grievous, displeasing, and hateful a person's troubles, blasphemous temptations, doubts, and fears are to him, the more assured he may be that they will not condemn him, because they are not loved or cherished sins.

All our troubles are under God's governance. It is far better to be at His disposal than at our own or that of our closest friends. He has promised that all things work together for good to those who love God and are called according to His purpose. A delight in God and in goodness, together with a joyful, praising spirit born of trust in God's love through Christ, is far better than grief and tears that only wash away some filth. Such delight lets in love, joy, and thankfulness — the true evangelical virtues that resemble the heavenly state.

Reflect on these truths, and they will heal you.

If melancholy has already taken hold, then, beyond what has been said, other remedies must be applied. The difficulty is great because the condition makes people self-satisfied, unreasonable, willful, and unruly. They rarely admit the illness is in their bodies; they insist it is only in their souls. They will think all their thoughts and actions are reasonable; or, if they admit otherwise, they plead disability: "We cannot think or act differently than we do."

If any reason remains, I offer further advice. What they cannot do for themselves, their friends must do for them as far as possible. To this I will add:

Keep in mind that, amid confusing and troubling thoughts, your understanding is likely not as sound or as strong as that of others. Do not be willful and self-satisfied, assuming your thoughts are more accurate than theirs. Trust wiser people and let them guide you.

Ask yourself, "Do I know any minister or friend wiser than I am?" If you answer no, consider how foolishly proud you are. If you answer yes, ask that minister or friend what they think of your condition, and trust their judgment rather than your own distorted perceptions.

Do your troubles do you more good or more harm? Do they make you more or less able to believe in and love God, to rejoice in Him, and to praise Him? If they seem contrary to all that is good, you may be sure they come from the devil's temptations and are pleasing to him. Will you cherish or defend Satan's work when it plainly fights against both you and God?

Avoid dwelling on your thoughts. For now, do not engage in deep or excessive contemplation. Long meditation may be a duty for some, but it is not for you—just as it is not a person's duty to attend church with a broken leg or a dislocated foot. Such a person must rest and allow the limb to be set and strengthened.

You can live in the faith and fear of God without subjecting yourself to deep, disturbing thoughts. If someone will not heed this advice, friends must pull them away from melancholic musings and set them to other activities.

Do not spend too much time alone. Be in pleasant, cheerful company instead, because solitude encourages brooding. Also limit the time you spend in private prayer and take part more in public prayer with others.

Turn your thoughts to the most excellent things. Do not fixate on yourself and your troubled heart; even the best among us can find much distressing material there. Just as millstones wear themselves out when they grind without grain, so the thoughts of those who do not contemplate better things wear themselves away.

If you have any control over your thoughts, compel them to dwell on these four subjects:

1. The infinite goodness of God — He is more full of love than the sun is full of light.

2. The immeasurable love of Christ in the redemption of humanity, and the sufficiency of His sacrifice and merits.

3. The free covenant and offer of grace, which grants pardon and life to all who do not prefer the pleasure of sin to it, nor obstinately refuse it to the end.

4. The inconceivable glory and joy that the blessed share with Christ, which God has promised by His oath and seal to all who accept the covenant of grace and are willing to be saved and governed by Christ. These thoughts will ease melancholy and fear.

5. Do not grow used to complaining. Speak often instead of the great mercies of God that you have received. Can you deny them? If not, are they not more worthy of your conversation than your present sufferings?

Do not let everyone know about your troubles; complaining only feeds them and discourages others. Share them only with trusted advisors and friends. Make it a habit to speak frequently of God's love and the riches of His grace; this will help divert and sweeten your sour thoughts.

6. When you pray, spend the greater part of your time in thanksgiving and praise to God. If you cannot do it with the joy you desire, give

thanks as best you can. You may not control your comforts, but you do control your tongue.

Do not say that, unless you have a praising heart and are a child of God, you are unfit for thanksgiving and praise. Every person, whether good or bad, is obligated to praise God and to be thankful for what they have received. They must do so to the best of their ability rather than leave it undone.

Many Christians lack assurance of adoption. Should they therefore refrain from all praise and thanksgiving? No. Doing it to the best of your ability is the way to grow. Thanksgiving stirs up thankfulness in the heart.

If you object, remember what the devil aims at and what he gains from your melancholy: he seeks to turn you away from all thankfulness to God and from even mentioning His love and goodness in your praises.

7. When troubling or blasphemous thoughts are thrust into your mind by Satan, do not entertain them or be overly troubled by them. First, use the reason and strength you have left to resolutely cast them out. Then redirect your thoughts to something else. Do not say, "I cannot." If you cannot command and turn away your thoughts otherwise, rise up and seek company or engage in activities that will divert you.

Consider what you would do if you heard someone in the street reviling you or an atheist speaking against God. Would you stand there and listen or argue with them? Wouldn't you prefer to walk away and disdain to engage? In your situation, when Satan injects ugly, despairing, or murmuring thoughts, turn away from them to other thoughts or tasks.

If you cannot manage this on your own, tell a friend when the temptation arises. It is their duty, as someone who cares for you, to distract you with other conversations or activities, or to encourage you to seek diverting company.

Do not be overly troubled by the temptation. Mental distress keeps troubling thoughts in your memory and makes them worse, just as the pain of a sore draws blood and energy to the area. This is Satan's design: he gives you troubling thoughts and then creates more by causing you to be troubled by them.

Thus, one thought and trouble lead to another, like waves following one another on the sea. Being tempted is common to all of us. I mentioned the idolatry to which Christ was tempted. When you experience such thoughts, thank God that Satan cannot force you to love them or to consent to them.

8. Remember the comforting evidence you carry within you: your sin is not damning so long as you feel that you do not love it, but rather hate it and are weary of it. Few sinners find as little pleasure in their sin as melancholic individuals do, nor do they have much desire to hold onto it; only beloved sins lead to ruin.

Be sure to avoid idleness and take up some consistent, lawful work as much as your physical strength allows. Idleness is a constant temptation; labor is a duty. Idleness is the devil's playground for temptation and unproductive, distracting thoughts. Work benefits others and ourselves; both our souls and bodies require it.

You must labor six days and not eat the bread of idleness (Proverbs 31). God has made this our duty, and He will bless us in His appointed way. I have seen severe, despairing melancholy cured and transformed into godly cheerfulness, primarily through consistent diligence in family and work responsibilities. This focus diverts thoughts from temptation and leaves the devil no opportunity. It pleases God when done in obedience and purifies the troubled spirit.

Many poor people live in want, with wives and children who also feel the burden. One might think they would be overwhelmed with grief and worry, yet few of them fall into melancholy. Labor keeps the body healthy and leaves no time for melancholic thoughts. In contrast, in cities like London, many women who do not engage in physical work but live in idleness—especially when they fall from wealth to poverty—become miserable, constantly troubled, and on the brink of distraction from discontent and a restless mind.

If you will not be persuaded to engage in work, then your friends should encourage you to do so, if they are able.

If the devil masquerades as an angel of light and tells you that work merely distracts your thoughts from God, and that worldly tasks are unholy and suited only for worldly people—remind him that Adam, in his innocence, was tasked with tending and keeping his garden; Noah, who had the whole world, was a farmer; Abraham, Isaac, and Jacob cared for sheep and cattle; Paul was a tentmaker; and Christ Himself is believed to have worked in His supposed father's trade, fishing with His disciples. Paul says that idleness is disorderly conduct: "If anyone will not work, neither shall he eat" (2 Thessalonians 3:10-11). God created both soul and body, and He has commanded both to work.

If Satan attempts to compel you to engage in excessively long private prayer beyond your capacity, remember that even sickness excuses the sick from duties they cannot perform; your condition does the same. The Spirit Himself makes intercession for us with groanings which cannot be uttered (Romans 8:26). If you have privacy away from others, I advise you to sing a psalm of praise to God, such as the twenty-third or the one hundred thirty-third psalm. This will elevate your spirit to a kind of holy affection that is far more acceptable to God and aligns better with the hopes of a believer than your troubled complaints.

9. The Responsibility of Friends and Relatives

I am not yet finished discussing the responsibilities of those who care for distressed, melancholic individuals, particularly the duties of husbands towards their wives (as this condition is much more common among women than men). When the illness prevents them from helping themselves, most of their support, under God, must come from others. This support can be categorized into two types:

1. In prudent behavior towards them;

2. In medicine and diet—a combination of both.

A significant part of their recovery lies in pleasing them and avoiding, as far as is lawful, anything that displeases them. Displeasure greatly contributes to the illness. A husband with such a wife is obliged to do his best to help her—out of love, because of his marital bond, and for his own peace.

It is a serious weakness in some men that, when they have wives who are naturally emotionally sensitive, melancholic, or unstable and therefore willful and resistant to reason, they respond with anger and so provoke her further. You married her for better or for worse, in sickness and in health. If you chose someone who, like a child, needs everything she cries for and must be treated gently, you must accommodate that. Bear the burden you have chosen so as not to make it heavier for yourself. Your anger and bitterness toward someone who cannot control her unpleasant behavior is a far more inexcusable fault and folly than hers, since she lacks the reasoning ability you possess.

If you know of any lawful ways to please her—by conversation, companionship, clothing, room arrangements, or attention—provide them. If you know what displeases her, remove it. I am not speaking of those so distracted they must be restrained by force, but of those who are sad and melancholic. If you can find a way to put her into a pleased state, you may help cure her.

As much as possible, divert her from troubling thoughts. Keep her engaged in other conversations and activities. Interrupt her musings with gentle insistence and do not leave her alone for long. Find suitable company for her, or take her to it.

Do not allow her to be idle; instead, encourage or guide her toward pleasant activities that occupy both body and mind. If she enjoys reading, limit the time and avoid books unsuitable for her. Have someone read to her rather than letting her read alone. Useful and agreeable histories or chronicles, news of important events, or books by Dr. Sibbes may help to divert her.

Frequently remind her of the great, comforting truths of the gospel. Read uplifting and informative books to her, and live with her in a loving, cheerful manner.

Select a skilled, prudent minister of Christ for her, both for private counsel and for public ministry. Choose someone experienced in such matters—peaceable, not contentious, free from error or fondness for strange opinions. He should be judicious in preaching and praying rather than excessively emotional, except when earnestly urging the comforting doctrines of the gospel, where fervor is welcome. Above all, pick someone she respects and will listen to.

Work diligently to convince her how great a wrong it is to the God of infinite love and mercy, and to a Savior who has shown His love so wonderfully, to think less of Him than she would of a friend or even a moderate enemy. It would be shameful ingratitude and injury to suppose that One who has risked His life for her and given her everything has intended it all against her, designed harm for her, and did not love her. How have God and our Savior deserved this?

Many who say they do not suspect God but only themselves are merely hiding their misery behind this misunderstanding. They deny God's greatest mercies. Although they would gladly accept Christ and grace, they do not believe that the God who offers them will actually give them. Instead, they imagine He will, without remedy, condemn a poor soul who desires to please Him and would rather have His grace than all the sinful pleasures of the world.

Take her out often into unfamiliar company. She will usually show respect toward strangers, and new faces can be a helpful distraction, especially if she is able to travel.

Encourage her to comfort others who are in deeper distress than she is. This will remind her that her situation is not unique and will prompt reflection on her own condition as she helps others. One of the chief means that alleviated my fears about my own soul nearly forty-eight years ago was often comforting others who shared similar doubts; their lives reassured me of their sincerity.

It could also be an interesting diversion to send her someone who holds views she strongly opposes to debate with her. As she sharpens her wits to convince and refute that person, it may redirect her thoughts away from her own distress. A melancholy patient of a colleague — who was a papist — found relief when the Reformation came to the country by engaging in fervent disputes against it. A better cause may yield even better results.

10. Medical Care

If other means do not work, do not neglect medicine. Even though some may resist it, believing the illness to be purely of the mind, they must be persuaded or, if necessary, compelled to take it. I have known a woman who was deeply melancholic and for a long time refused to speak, to take medicine, or to allow her husband to leave the room. With that confinement and sorrow, he died; she was later cured by medicine administered forcibly through a pipe.

If it were possession by the devil, as some believe, medicine might still drive him out. If you cure the melancholy, the devil's influence is removed and he loses the means by which he operates. Cure the anger, and the devil's angry actions cease. He works through our bodily humors.

Choose a physician specifically skilled in treating this condition and who has successfully cured many others. Avoid women, ignorant boastful individuals, young inexperienced men, and hasty, overly ambitious people who do not take time to understand the patient's temperament and illness. Instead, select experienced and cautious practitioners.

Medicinal remedies and theological remedies were not typically administered by the same practitioner. However, where mental and physical ailments are closely intertwined, I believe it appropriate that one who is skilled should attend to both. My advice is that those who can consult an older, skilled, experienced, honest, careful, and cautious physician should do so, and avoid using any of the medicines I will mention—or any other prescriptions—without their physician's guidance. There is such a great variety of bodily conditions, ages, incidental factors, and different roots and causes for the same symptoms that the same medicine may cure one person while harming another. It may cure the same person at one time and harm them at another. Skill in administering the medicine is an essential part of the cure, not merely the medicine itself.

Many are so poor they cannot afford a physician, and the high cost of doctors and pharmacists discourages those without money from seeking help. They often turn to women who sell concoctions. Many in rural areas are far from skilled physicians, and an increasing number of quacks and inexperienced doctors venture forth without fully understanding the body or the illness. The dangers of overdoing things and taking rash risks lead to many deaths. For these reasons I will give a few safe, inexpensive remedies that the poor can prepare themselves and that will not upset their stomachs too much—though I risk criticism from some physicians. I am not a physician myself, but I see many younger ones who take far greater risks once they obtain a license, often to the detriment of their patients' finances and health.

The condition known as melancholy primarily affects the spirits. Its disorder renders the spirits unfit for their roles in serving the imagination, understanding, memory, and affections. Consequently, when the spirits are disordered, the process of thinking malfunctions; it is like an inflamed eye or a sprained or dislocated foot—it cannot perform its proper function.

Sometimes healthy individuals suddenly fall into melancholy from a fright, the death of a friend, a significant loss, or distressing news. This shows it does not always arise from the humor called melancholy or from any prior illness.

The very act of the mind can suddenly disrupt the affections and disturb the spirits. Over time, these disturbed spirits can taint the blood that carries them, and that tainted blood can eventually harm the organs and systems through which it flows. Thus the disease, which begins in the senses and soul, first affects the spirits, then the humors, and finally the body, producing a concurrent illness of both soul and body.

The devil has another remedy for the sad and melancholic that differs from those I have prescribed. This remedy involves rejecting all belief in the immortality of the soul and the life to come, or at least avoiding all thoughts of it. It encourages viewing religion as a superstitious, unnecessary fancy and mocking the warnings of Scripture. It urges escape through plays, card games, and drinking.

Honest recreational activities can be helpful for melancholic people, if they could be persuaded to take part. But this satanic remedy resembles a witch's bargain with the devil: it promises much and delivers only shame and utter misery. The mirth it produces ends, if uncorrected by timely repentance, in incurable sorrow.

The stronghold of Satan in the hearts of sinners is firmly maintained when they are at peace. But when those sinners squander time, mercy, and hope, they must face death—and there will be no remedy. Going merrily and unbelievingly into hell, despite all of God's calls and warnings, will not lessen the torment. Leaving this world weighed down by sin, ignorant of its purpose, and unrepentant before God's justice for despising Christ and grace will bring a sorrowful close to all their joy.

For "There is no peace," says the LORD, "for the wicked." (Isaiah 48:22, 57:21) Yet Christ assures His mourners, "Blessed are those who mourn, For they shall be comforted." (Matthew 5:4) He also said, "Most assuredly, I say to you that you will weep and lament, but the world will rejoice; and you will be sorrowful, but your sorrow will be turned into joy." (John 16:20)

Solomon recognized that it is better to go to the house of mourning than to go to the house of feasting; that sorrow is better than laughter; that the heart of the wise is in the house of mourning, while the heart of fools is in the house of mirth (Ecclesiastes 7:2-4) — yet the holy joy of faith and hope surpasses all.

END

The original text concluded with some primitive diagnostics and recipes from the 17th century, which have not been included in this print due to being outdated.

www.ingramcontent.com/pod-product-compliance
Lightning Source LLC
Chambersburg PA
CBHW021132080526
44587CB00012B/1249